# On a train jour

# INTRODUCTION

Almost everyone loves to take a train journey. As well as the excitement of reaching your destination – perhaps you are going on holiday to the seaside – railway stations and the trains themselves are full of fascinating things to see from the moment you get to the station, before you start your trip, to arriving at the other end. At a big station, there is all the hustle and bustle of travel, as well as a range of shops to browse around, and the various kinds of refreshments to be had. You might use a local train just to get to school, or you could use a service to take you from one end of the country to the other. You can use a laptop on some trains, and you can often find buffet carriages or trolleys selling food and drink on board, including full meals on those trains that have a restaurant car.

There are now nearly 30 separate train companies operating regular passenger and freight trains on Britain's national railway system. And there are underground lines and metros, special trains and steam railways, too. So look out for a wonderful variety of trains, locomotives and carriages, all in their different colours, as you travel the country.

And, as you travel (sometimes at speeds of up to 125mph (200km/h)), there is so much to see provided you keep your eyes open. It's fun to find out about the world as it rushes by, and you'll be surprised by all the fascinating things you'll discover. Of course, if you travel by car, you must not distract the driver but, on a train journey, all the family can join in the i-SPY fun.

## How to use your i-SPY book

There are so many things you could look out for on a train journey that it's hard to know where to begin, what to include, or what to leave out. Your i-SPY on a Train Journey book takes you from your arrival at the station, through the station itself and along the journey to your destination. Many entries in the book are activities you'll do, others are things you'll see. Score points for either seeing or doing.

You need 1000 points to send off for your i-SPY certificate (see page 64) but that is not too difficult because there are masses of points in every book. Each entry has a star or circle and points value beside it. The stars represent harder to spot entries. As you make each i-SPY, write your score in the circle or star. For entries where there is a question, double your score if you can answer it. Answers are shown on page 63.

**Points: 5**

### SIGNPOST

This sign shows the way to the station and to the city centre.

### FOUNTAIN

**Points: 10**

Some stations have elaborate fountains in their forecourt.

**Points: 10**

### STATION CANOPY

You might arrive to find yourself under a canopy which protects travellers from the rain.

## STATION CAR PARK

Many railway stations have large car parks. Double points if the station is a Parkway – a station built specially to serve motorists from a wide area.

**Points: 5**

## PAY AND DISPLAY

After parking, be sure to pay and display!

**Points: 5**

## MOTORCYCLE PARKING

As well as cars, stations have places to park motorcycles...

**Points: 5**

## BICYCLE PARKING

...and for bicycles.

**Points: 5**

## STATION SIGN

Outside the station, there is usually a large sign showing its name, often with the famous double arrow symbol.

 **Points: 5**

## STATION NAME BOARD

All stations have name boards on the platform so that travellers arriving can see where they are.

 **Points: 5**

## KEEP BACK SIGN

Keep well back from the platform edge and behind the yellow line

Fast-moving trains travel through some stations. It is important to stand well back from the edge of the platform and observe the safety instructions.

**Points: 5**

## TICKET SIGN

You will need to buy a valid ticket for your journey. You may have to pay a penalty if you don't have a valid ticket.

 **Points: 5**

### NO SMOKING

All stations now have a no-smoking policy...

 **Points: 5**

### CCTV

...and most have security cameras.

**Points: 5**

### ACCESSIBLE BOARDING

Many stations have facilities for wheelchair users...

**Points: 5**

### HELP POINT

...and if you need to ask for help it can be found at the touch of a button!

 **Points: 10**

### Points: 20

### PLATFORM 9 ¾

This very famous platform might not really exist! However, if you're in King's Cross station in London, keep your eyes peeled...

### RURAL STATION

### Points: 10

This is a traditional wayside country station. These small stations found in the countryside are quite different to the huge stations you'll find in cities that are packed with shops and cafés.

### Points: 10

### FLOWER DISPLAYS

Some stations, particularly those in more rural locations, have beautiful flower displays.

## WAITING ROOM

Whilst waiting for a train, you can always use the waiting room.

 **Points: 5**

## READY TO DEPART

This platform is almost empty as the last passengers get ready to board.

**Points: 5**

## WEIGHING MACHINE

Arena Photo UK / Shutterstock.com

You may need to weigh your luggage (or yourself).

 **Points: 10**

## CYCLISTS LOADING

You can sometimes leave your bike in special cycle parks on the platform, but if you want to take  your bike with you, look out for the special loading point. Some trains have carriages designated for carrying bikes.

**Points: 10**

30 Points: 30    Top Spot!    **LONGEST NAME**

This is a special station that is found on the island of Anglesey in Wales. It is the station for the village that has the longest place name in Europe and second longest place name in the World!

## TRADITIONAL OVERBRIDGE

**Points: 5**

Many stations have a footbridge linking the platforms.

 **Points: 5**

## ENCLOSED OVERBRIDGE

This bridge is enclosed, keeping you dry when it rains.

## ROAD BRIDGE

**Points: 5**

Here you can see a road bridge over the rails.

**Points: 10**

### TRAVEL CENTRE

Large stations always have a travel centre where you can buy tickets and make reservations.

### INFORMATION STAND

**Points: 10**

You can get all the information you need to plan your journey.

**Points: 10**

### INFORMATION BOOTH

Many stations have an information booth where you can ask for assistance.

## CONNECTION BOARD

**Points: 5** 5

If you have to change trains to arrive at your final destination, you'll need to look carefully for which station you need to change trains at, and how much time you will have between getting off one train and getting on the next.

5 **Points: 5**

## SELF-SERVICE TICKET MACHINE

Many stations have self-service ticket machines where you can purchase tickets without having to go to the ticket office or collect tickets that you have preordered.

IR Stone / Shutterstock.com

**5** — **Points: 5**

### TICKET COUNTER

You may choose to speak to someone and buy your ticket…

### TICKET QUEUE

**Points: 5** **5**

…which may involve standing in a queue.

**5** — **Points: 5**

### STAFF

Staff are always willing to offer help and assistance.

5 Points: 5

Train stations usually have large digital information boards that give details of all the upcoming arrivals and departures. On these boards you can also find out which platform your train will depart from, which stations your train will call at, and whether it is on time, delayed, or even cancelled.

**Points: 10**

## STATION CLOCK

Some stations have clocks outside...

## CONCOURSE CLOCK

**Points: 10**

...some have analogue clocks inside on the concourse...

Paul Wishart / Shutterstock.com

**Points: 10**

## COMBINATION CLOCK

...and some stations have a combination of digital and analogue clocks to make sure you don't miss your train!

Thomas Barrat / Shutterstock.com

**Points: 10**
double with answser

### RAILWAY POLICE

Britain's railways have had their own independent police force since the very beginning. Originally, railway police officers also acted as signallers and controlled the movement of trains. Even today, some railway staff refer to the signaller as 'bobby'.

*Do you know why police officers are called bobbies?*

### FLOOR ENGRAVING

**Points: 10**

In some stations, you might see a plaque or engraving on the floor. They often contain famous quotes.

**Points: 15**

### STATUE

Some stations have a statue in their concourse. The statue in the photo is of Paddington Bear who was famously found in Paddington station when he arrived in London from Peru.

Aija Lehtonen / Shutterstock.com

16

## GLASS ROOF

This station roof in York is huge. The top section is made of glass, allowing lots of natural light to shine through into the station.

10 **Points: 10**

## TILED SIGN

chamstr / Shutterstock.com

This is an example of when old meets new. Note the old tiled station sign and the modern version underneath.

15 **Points: 15**

## METAL SEAT

You can find seats to sit on while you wait for your train...

10 **Points: 10**

## TOURIST INFORMATION

...or pick up some local information.

10 **Points: 10**

## POSTBOX

You can post a letter...

 **Points: 10**

## PERMIT TO TRAVEL

...or get a permit to travel.

 **Points: 10**

## TOILET

Stations always have facilities available for use.

**Points: 5**

## MEETING POINT

Here's where you can meet your friends and family at the end of their journey.

 **Points: 10**

**Points: 20**

## COURTESY BUGGY

A number of main-line stations have courtesy buggies like this one to help travellers who need assistance getting themselves and their luggage to and from the train.

## LUGGAGE TROLLEY

**Points: 10**

There are always plenty of self-help luggage trolleys to save carrying heavy suitcases and bags by hand.

**Points: 10**

## WHEELED SUITCASE

Some suitcases come complete with their own wheels.

**Points: 10**

10

### ESCALATOR

Change level on an escalator...

### LIFT

### WHEELCHAIR ACCESS

Richard Thornton / Shutterstock.com

Some trains have low level entry for wheelchair access.

**Points: 15**

...or in a lift.

10 **Points: 10**

**Points: 5**

**MODERN SEAT**

It's always nice to be able to take the weight off your feet and sit down whilst waiting for a train. Modern seats are made from metal and look like this.

**NEWSPAPER**

**Points: 5**

You can always read a newspaper or magazine whilst you wait…

**Points: 5**

**PHONE CALL**

…or make a phone call.

### TICKET PUNCH

The guard may punch your ticket.

*Why does he do this?*

**Points: 5**
double with answer

### SAY GOODBYE

You may be leaving someone special at the station.

**Points: 10**

### ATTENDANT

You may wish to check with the attendant that this is the right train.

**Points: 10**

### BOARD THE TRAIN

Lee Prince / Shutterstock.com

There is usually a rush to get on board.

**Points: 5**

**10** Points: 10

**WAVE GOODBYE**

You may be waving goodbye to someone.

**WHISTLE**

Points: 20

Once everyone is onboard the whistle is blown, a signal is given and the train departs!

**10** Points: 10

**TRAIN DRIVER**

If you are lucky you may even see the train driver.

### RESTAURANT CAR

Many intercity trains carry a restaurant car where travellers can enjoy a full meal, with wine, while on the move.

**Points: 10**

### CHEF

A fully-trained chef will prepare your meal for you...

**Points: 10**

### TABLE SERVICE

...and will even serve it to your table.

**Points: 10**

### TEA AND COFFEE

You may, however, just fancy tea, coffee or juice.

**Points: 10**

**Points: 5**

**BUFFET CAR**

Hot snacks and a wide variety of light refreshments are available from the buffet car.

**NEWSPAPER**

**Points: 10**

Sometimes you will be able to buy a newspaper on board the train – they'll usually be found in the buffet car.

**Points: 10**

**TROLLEY SERVICE**

A trolley service brings a selection of drinks and snacks to you at your seat.

cowardlion / Shutterstock.com

## Points: 15

**WIFI**

It's easy to stay in touch on a train journey. Many stations now offer WiFi facilities...

**MOBILE PHONES**

## Points: 10

...for mobile phones...

## Points: 15

**LAPTOPS**

....and laptops. Some business professionals have meetings while the train is moving.

**Points: 15**

## WORKING ON THE TRAIN

Many trains these days have a WiFi connection and electric sockets to plug in electrical appliances. This means that many people, especially those who use trains to commute to work each day, take the opportunity to do some work while travelling.

## PLAYING GAMES

**Points: 15**

It doesn't have to be work. You can play on the train as well!

## SEATING

**Points: 5** for each

See how many of these seat configurations you can spot.

**Points: 10**

**FIRST CLASS**

First class seats usually have headrest covers bearing the name of the train company operating the service.

**CURTAINS**

**Points: 15**

If you feel you need a rest, you can draw the curtains!

 **Points: 15**

**SEAT RESERVATION**

It's a good idea to reserve your seat so that you know you'll be able to sit down for the duration of your train journey.

### EMERGENCY INSTRUCTIONS

In the event of an emergency these posters tell you exactly what to do.

 **Points: 10**

### ALARM HANDLE

The alarm handle must only ever be pulled in case of an emergency. It sends a message to the driver to stop the train.

**Points: 10**

### AUTOMATIC DOORS

Some trains have automatic doors. These open at the push of a button when the train is in a station.

 **Points: 10**

### TOILET

A toilet with washbasin, soap and towels so you can freshen up on a long journey.

 **Points: 5**

### LUGGAGE RACK

Luggage racks can be found above the seats and at the end of carriages.

**Points: 5**

### QUIET CARRIAGE

Many trains now have a dedicated quiet carriage. This is for people who wish to travel in peace, so no music or telephones in here please!

**Points: 15**

### ELECTRIC SUPPLY

If you want to work (or play) on the train you may need an electricity supply.

 **Points: 10**

**WINDMILL**

Top Spot!    Points: 35    35

Windmills use the power of the wind to turn their sails. They can be used to grind grain into flour, pump water or to generate elctricity.

**Points: 15**

### POPPY FIELD

As your train is travelling through the countryside, keep a look out for poppy fields. These fields look like huge red carpets.

### GAS HOLDER

**Points: 5**

A gas holder, sometimes called a gasometer, is where natural gas is often stored.

**Points: 10**

### POWER STATION

You may pass a power station on your train journey – this one has four big cooling towers.

**5** Points: 5

## CHURCH

Keep an eye out for churches, and sometimes even cathedrals, with their high steeples and towers.

## RIVER

Points: 5 **5**

Trains often pass by rivers when travelling through the countryside.

**5** Points: 5

## MOTORWAY BRIDGE

Sometimes the train line goes over a motorway or a dual carriageway like this one.

**Points: 10**

### WIND TURBINE

Wind turbines are a common sight these days, and you may see some through the window of the train.

### ELECTRICITY PYLONS

**Points: 5**

Electricity pylons are everywhere so you're bound to see one on your journey.

**Points: 25**   Top Spot!

### DEER

If you're lucky, you might catch a glimpse of a deer if your train is passing through the countryside or near to a deer park.

### CASTLE

**Points: 15**

Look out for castles and castle ruins – Corfe Castle in Dorset (in the photo) can be seen from Corfe Castle train station.

**Points: 15**

### HOT-AIR BALLOON

Sometimes you can see hot-air balloons from the train window. If you're travelling around dawn or dusk, keep a special eye out for them – they're often flown around these times, when the thermals they float on are more stable.

## CANAL

This train is passing a canal.

 **Points: 15**

## FERRY

This train is at a station which serves a harbour and a large ferry boat can be seen behind it.

 **Points: 20**

## HARBOUR

The line may pass a harbour.

 **Points: 15**

## PIER

Or you may pass along the seafront and spot a pier.

 **Points: 15**

*Railway lines are carried across valleys, rivers and roads by a variety of bridges and viaducts.*

### VIADUCT

**Points: 15**

15

This impressive viaduct is constructed of stone and has many arches.

10

**Points: 10**

### RIVER BRIDGE

These trains are crossing the River Thames in London. Do you know which station they are leaving from?

### Points: 5

**BUFFER STOP**

Where a line ends in a station or at a siding, there will be a buffer stop. These are often painted red and may have one or more red lights.

**STOP SIGN**

### Points: 10

Sometimes lines may be blocked for engineering work and a temporary stop board will be placed on the line.

### Points: 15

**NOT TO BE MOVED**

'Not to be moved' boards are used when the train is being cleaned or if an engineer is working on the train.

*There are two main types of signals used on the UK railway network, colour light signals and mechanical signals (often called semaphores).*

 **Points: 5**

## JUNCTION SIGNAL

These have an arm mounted on a post that can be moved up and down to indicate stop (horizontal) or proceed (raised or lowered). The arms can be red or yellow depending on the function of the signal and there may be more than one arm if there is a junction ahead.

## DISTANT SIGNAL

**Points: 15**

This is a distant signal. It shows caution, which means that the driver will have to stop at the next signal.

 **Points: 15**

## TRADITIONAL SHUNTING SIGNAL

This is a shunting signal. This one is showing stop. The disc turns 45 degrees to show proceed. Signals like this are used to allow trains to move into sidings or to cross from one track to another.

**Points: 10**

## TWO-ASPECT SIGNAL

A red signal tells the driver to stop.

## MODERN SHUNTING SIGNAL

**Points: 15**

This is a modern shunting signal. Two red lights means stop. Two white lights at 45 degrees means proceed.

### Points: 10

### TRESPASSING SIGN

You will find this sign at locations near railway lines such as level crossings.

### ELECTRIFIED LINES SIGN

### Points: 10

This sign is found near electrified lines. The cables carry 25,000 volts therefore staff and passengers must keep well away from them.

### Points: 25    Top Spot!

### LIMITED CLEARANCE SIGN

Maintenance crews may have to work on the line while trains are running. When a train approaches, they have to get to a 'position of safety'. In some areas, such as on bridges and in cuttings, there is not much room by the side of the track. This is where you will find a 'limited clearance' sign.

*Like roads, railway lines have varying speed limits. Trains may have to slow down at different locations such as junctions, crossovers, and sharp bends.*

 **Points: 10**

## TRIANGULAR SPEED RESTRICTIONS

This is a triangular advanced warning sign. It tells the driver that the speed indicated applies to the line ahead.

## CIRCULAR SPEED RESTRICTIONS

**Points: 15**

This circular warning sign indicates the point where the speed limit starts.

 **Points: 20**

## CUT-OUT SPEED RESTRICTIONS

Before the modern circular and triangular warning signs were introduced, metal signs with cut-out numerals were used.

*There are two types of electrified line in the UK. A third rail (750 volts DC) outside the main running rails is used on many lines south of London. The other system uses high voltage overhead power lines (25,000 volts AC) known as catenary.*

## Points: 15

### OVERHEAD WIRES

On single and many double-track lines, single masts are usually used to support the overhead wires which zigzag to even out wear on the pantograph's collector strips.

### PANTOGRAPH

## Points: 20

This is a pantograph on the roof of a train. It collects power from the lines above the train, which helps the train gather and maintain speed.

## Points: 15

### HEADSPAN

Where there are multiple lines, structures such as this one, called a headspan, are used.

**Points: 20**

**THIRD RAIL**

This train in Merseyside is using its 'shoes' to pick up power from the third rail which you can see on the outside of the running rails.

## HIGH SPEED TRAIN

**Points: 15**

Introduced by British Rail in 1976, the diesel High Speed Train (HST) is still widely used across the country on long distance services. These trains have a top speed of 125mph and have a power car at either end to pull and push the train.

**Points: 20**

## CLASS 390 PENDOLINO

This is a Class 390 Pendolino. These electric trains tilt which means that they can go faster around curves than normal trains and cut journey times. The tilting mechanism makes it more comfortable for passengers. Their maximum speed is currently 125mph although they were designed for 140mph.

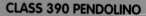

**Points: 20**

### CLASS 91 ELECTRIC

This is a class 91 electric locomotive. At the other end of the train is a carriage with a driving cab. The locomotive stays at one end of the train and is controlled from the other end of the train when travelling in the other direction. This is called a push-pull train.

i4cool7 / Shutterstock.com

### CLASS 220 VOYAGER

**Points: 20**

This is a Class 220 Voyager train. These trains and similar Class 221 and 222 units were built to replace older trains on routes across the country. The Class 221 trains are designed to tilt like the Class 390 Pendolino and have a top speed of 125mph.

Paul J Martin / Shutterstock.com

# DIESEL MULTIPLE UNITS

*These trains have no separate locomotive but have diesel or electrically powered carriages with a cab at each end. They normally have their number on the front of the cab. The first three digits are the class number.*

**Points: 15**

## CLASS 185 DESIRO

The Class 185 Desiro has an engine in each carriage, but they do not all need to be used for the whole journey especially if the train is coasting downhill.

## CLASS 170 TURBOSTAR

**Points: 15**

The Class 170 Turbostar units consist of either two or three carriages. This one is taking passengers to Leicester.

**Points: 20**

## CLASS 143

The Class 143 units and the similar Class 142 were introduced in the 1980s. They were built as low-cost trains and reused many items, such as the seats from buses built by the same companies.

**Points: 15**

### CLASS 375 ELECTROSTAR

The Class 375 Electrostar units are used for commuter services in the south of England along with similar units of Classes 357, 376 and 377.

### CLASS 395

**Points: 15**

The Class 395 140mph trains are Britain's fastest domestic trains. The dual-voltage units were built in Japan for commuter services from London St Pancras to Kent.

**Points: 15**

### CLASS 350

The modern Class 350 units are part of the Desiro family of trains. They are used on commuter services in London and the south-east and also on the west coast main line to Birmingham, Crewe and Liverpool. Like the Electrostar, they can be configured to use overhead or third rail power.

*Today, the vast majority of passenger trains are multiple-unit trains that do not have a locomotive. However, locomotives are still used on some passenger routes.*

## CLASS 08 SHUNTER

**Points: 15**

15

This is a Class 08 Shunter. These were once the most numerous locomotives on the network as nearly 1000 of them were built. They have a very low top speed of 15mph and can easily be identified by their yellow and black 'wasp' stripes on the cab and nose end.

10 **Points: 10**

## FREIGHT LOCOMOTIVE

First bought by EWS to replace the life-expired ex-British Rail ones, these diesel locomotives are the most common freight locomotives in use in Britain today.

## Points: 15

**SLEEPER TRAIN**

These 125mph diesel locomotives were built mainly to haul parcels and mail trains around the network. They are currently used to haul sleeper trains.

## Points: 20

**CLASS 92**

The Class 92s are the most modern and sophisticated electric locomotives on the network. They were built to haul international freight and overnight passenger trains from Britain to France.

# FREIGHT TRAINS

*Freight trains carry goods all over the country. They are not as fast as passenger trains so a lot of them run at night.*

## HOPPER WAGONS

This train has hopper wagons for carrying coal from collieries and docks to power stations to generate electricity.

 **Points: 15**

## CONTAINERS

This train is carrying containers from a port. Huge cranes load the containers from ships on to the wagons.

 **Points: 20**

## TANK WAGONS

**Points: 20**

This is a train of tank wagons which are used to carry liquids and powders. These ones are carrying oil from a refinery.

**Points: 10**

EUROSTAR

Eurostar™ operates from London's St Pancras International station and trains transport you to either Paris or Brussels, travelling through the Channel Tunnel at speeds of up to 300km/h (186mph) on a network of high-speed lines. The company launched the first of a new fleet of trains at the end of 2015. The 'Eurostar e320' is capable of carrying up to 900 passengers.

**Points: 25**    **Top Spot!**

**STATUE**

This is a statue of the former Poet Laureate, Sir John Betjeman, who helped save St Pancras station from redevelopment in the 1960s.

*As well as the Eurostar™, there are other ways to leave the country. There are train services to the major airports – here are three options.*

**Points: 15**

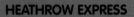

### HEATHROW EXPRESS

The Heathrow Express opened in 1998. It provides high-speed rail connections from central London's Paddington station to Heathrow Central (Terminals 1, 2, 3 and 4) and to Heathrow Terminal 5.

### GATWICK EXPRESS

**Points: 15**

The Gatwick Express was introduced in 1984. Trains run between London's Victoria station and Gatwick Airport every 15 minutes. The service takes around 30 minutes.

**Points: 15**

### STANSTED EXPRESS

Trains on the Stansted Express also run every 15 minutes but unlike the Gatwick Express, they stop at stations between the airport and the final destination, London's Liverpool Street station.

# STEAM TRAINS

*The last steam locomotives to be used for regular services on Britain's railways were withdrawn by British Rail in 1968. Many locomotives were then preserved by groups and individuals. Most of these are based on the preserved lines around the country but a number are permitted to run on the national rail network and can be seen hauling special trains.*

## DUCHESS OF SUTHERLAND

**Points: 20**
for any steam train

The Duchess of Sutherland is a preserved ex-LMS steam locomotive. The locomotive is seen here hauling a special from London King's Cross station to Norwich via Cambridge.

**Points: 30**   **Top Spot!**

## TORNADO

The first new steam train to be built in 50 years, the Tornado took 19 years to complete. Its maiden journey from Darlington to London's King's Cross was in February 2009.

*The London Underground was the world's first underground railway system – the first section opened in 1863.*

## ABOVE-GROUND STATION

This station is above ground level.

**Points: 5**

## UNDERGROUND SIGN

The famous circular logo of the London Underground has been used for nearly 100 years. Here it is used as a 'way out' sign.

Victor Moschek / Shutterstock.com

**Points: 5**

## UNDERGROUND STATION

Many of the platforms are deep under London and may require more than one escalator to reach ground level.

Chameleonseye / Shutterstock.com

*Do you know the deepest station on the network?*

**Points: 5**
double with answer

## UNDERGROUND PLATFORM

Some central London platforms are curved. As the train pulls into the station, there are sometimes gaps between the train and the edge of the platform. Be careful!

**Points: 5**

**10** **Points: 10**

**WAY OUT**

You may need to take the subway to another platform, or to the station exit.

**TAXI**

**Points: 5** **5**

You may need to take a taxi to reach your final destination…

**15** **Points: 15**

**FERRY TERMINAL**

…or you may need to catch a ferry to reach it!

**Points: 10**

**RAILWAY PUB**

A journey's end for some passengers may be a welcome drink at one of the many station inns which have a railway name.

**RAILWAY ARCHES**

**Points: 15**

The tracks into many city centre stations are carried above the streets on low viaducts. The spaces below the arches are often used as workshops and by restaurants that you might visit as you're leaving the station.

*All trains need to be maintained to ensure that they run smoothly and safely. The tracks also need to be constantly serviced. Most of the track work is carried out at night so as not to disrupt the system or service.*

**Points: 20**

### TRAIN BEING REPAIRED

For major repairs and refits, trains need to be taken to special maintenance depots.

### CLEANING

**Points: 15**

Trains, like cars, need to be regularly washed. You might see them going through a large 'train wash' or being done manually like this one.

*Apart from the usual passenger and freight trains there are other types of train and rail vehicles which you may see. These special vehicles are often painted yellow.*

**Points: 20**

### BREAKDOWN TRAIN

Breakdown trains are often old passenger carriages that have been converted to carry equipment that can be used to re-rail vehicles after a derailment.

### WATER-CANNON TRAIN

**Top Spot!** **Points: 25**

In the autumn, falling leaves can cause problems on the railway. To prevent these problems, water-cannon trains travel around the network spraying the track to clean off the leaves.

**Points: 20**

### HEAVY-DUTY CRANE

Heavy-duty cranes such as this one are used for lifting rail vehicles back on to the track when they have been removed for things like repairs.

nitirudI80 / Shutterstock.com

# LEVEL CROSSINGS

*A level crossing is where a road or footpath crosses a railway at the same level – always take care when using them.*

## MANUAL GATE

These traditional crossings have manually-controlled gates that are opened and closed by a crossing keeper every time a train passes.

**Points: 10**

## AUTOMATIC HALF-BARRIER

Crossings with automatic half-barriers have two barriers and therefore do not cover the whole road.

**Points: 10**

## FULL BARRIER

Full barrier crossings (manual and automated) have barriers across the whole width of the road.

**Points: 10**

## OPEN CROSSING

Open crossings have no barriers or gates across the road. They are used where quiet roads meet railway lines with very few trains.

**Points: 15**

# INDEX

**Answers: P16** Railway police: Bobbies are named after Sir Robert Peel (1788-1850), creator of the modern police force. **P22** Punch Ticket: The ticket is punched with a hole or mark to prevent it being used again. **P57** The deepest station is Hampstead, on the Northern Line, 58.52m (192ft) below ground level.

63

# i-SPY

## How to get your i-SPY certificate and badge

Let us know when you've become a super-spotter with 1000 points and we'll send you a special certificate and badge!

# HERE'S WHAT TO DO!

✓ Ask an adult to check your score.

✓ Visit www.collins.co.uk/i-SPY to apply for your certificate. If you are under the age of 13 you will need a parent or guardian to do this.

✓ We'll send your certificate via email and you'll receive a brilliant badge through the post!